IN THEIR
footsteps

CELEBRATING 25 YEARS OF BAKING
AT JERVAULX ABBEY

ACKNOWLEDGEMENTS

This book is dedicated to Major and Mrs W. V. Burdon,
without whom our journey would never have started.

A special thanks to Sue Firby, Carol's long-term friend.
She is the reason Carol came to Wensleydale and fell in love with the area.
Carol and Sue visited Jervaulx Abbey many times before meeting Ian.
Thanks also to George, Sue's husband. Together they have been a great
support to all the family.

Thanks to all our members of staff;
without them we wouldn't have been able to grow and develop.

Thanks to all those involved in creating this book at Meze Publishing,
and to photographer Tim Green. A long-term ambition has been fulfilled
with your dedication and help.

Thanks to all our suppliers, who have worked with us for a long time.
We wish them every success for the future.

As a family, we thank each other. We've always said that we are a team;
we have all worked together to support each other and will continue to do so.

CONTENTS

CLASSICS

NEWBIES

FREE FROM

RELISHES

FINISHING TOUCHES

WELCOME

WE, THE BURDON FAMILY, have had the pleasure of welcoming everyone to the Jervaulx Abbey Tearoom in North Yorkshire for twenty five years, since it opened in 1994. We have also had the enormous privilege, and responsibility, of continuing to preserve and celebrate the atmospheric abbey ruins through hard work and lots of delicious home baking and cooking in our family-run tearoom. This book is a wonderful way of celebrating what we've achieved, looking back at where we started, and moving forward to continue the care of Jervaulx Abbey for many generations to come. In Their Footsteps has been compiled to celebrate those twenty five years since we opened the tearoom's doors to the public.

Jervaulx is one of the largest privately owned Cistercian abbeys in the UK maintained solely by its owners, making our undertaking something of a feat of innovation and determination. Ian's father, known to all as Major Burdon, bought the land and what remained of the twelfth century abbey as a place to retire and return to his Yorkshire roots in 1971. The abbey's significant restoration project was managed by his sons, Rae and Ian, and then passed to Rae in 1980 following the Major's death. At the turn of the century, Ian purchased the abbey from Rae, and since then care of the abbey and its surrounding acres has been a labour of love for all of us. In 1993, Ian and Carol repurchased part of the estate and converted a couple of greenhouses into the Jervaulx Abbey Tearoom. Fifteen years later, daughters Gayle and Anna brought their talents and passions back home to develop the business further, and together we are now concentrating on managing the remaining monastic buildings that make up the beautiful abbey ruins.

It seemed like fate had stepped in when Ian and Carol met, as they shared a love of the area and of Jervaulx Abbey, and together were able to realise a long-held ambition of Carol's to open a tearoom founded on home baking. We opened the tearoom in 1994, having built it literally from the ground up on the site of a greenhouse and lean-to. Brick and slate from the original structures were used in the construction of the long light-filled building, connecting the new direction of the business to its long history. The idea was always to build up the business for the future, but equally for the girls to make their own decision about whether to become a part of it after they'd experienced life away from home. During that time, Carol baked for and ran the tearoom while Gayle got a qualification in hospitality and catering, and Anna went to university to study art. Both of their pursuits proved very useful at Jervaulx; Anna designed and made the information boards that surround the scale model of the abbey in the visitor centre, and Gayle started her own bespoke wedding and celebration cake business, Where The Ribbon Ends, which is now award-winning and continues to thrive following its move to bigger premises at Jervaulx. Anna ran the tearoom with Carol from 2010, picking up baking tricks and tips from her mum along the way.

Where The Ribbon Ends
at Jervaulx Abbey
Tearooms

CAKE

BE HAPPY
EAT
CAKE

THE TEAROOM'S REPUTATION GREW STEADILY right from the start, and as demand increased we enjoyed learning how to adapt and move with the times. We continued to diversify the business with the same family-oriented values at its core, such as the design and build of the Chapter House extension in 2014. This was planned as a private events venue, but was actually used almost daily to accommodate all our customers, and was especially popular for enjoying the award-winning afternoon teas that Carol and Anna developed around the same time, as well as group lunches for varied occasions, parties, wedding ceremonies and receptions. Focusing on home baking and cooking as a shared love, we brought lots of people to Jervaulx through the tearoom which helped our work at the abbey.

We have worked incredibly hard as a tight-knit unit to secure not only our future but the future of the abbey too. For us, it's a privilege to be responsible for something of such historical importance, and so we've stuck to an ethos that balances our need to make a living with preserving the very special feel of Jervaulx. The Honesty Box has been in place since Major Burdon introduced it in 1972, so people can visit anytime between dawn and dusk. Rather than information boards, we had an informative guide book produced which is designed to be read as you walk around, so you can learn as little or as much as you want with nothing to get in the way of a picturesque photo opportunity! And there are plenty of these to take advantage of, from mysterious nooks and crannies to grand archways and soaring walls. All this is adorned and framed by the profusion of greenery that has been allowed to flourish; a living thatch that in many cases has protected the stonework from weathering and creates beautiful, natural decoration of the ruins all year round. Over two hundred species of wild flowers, plants and trees were recorded in a 2009 survey at Jervaulx, some of which are now rare ancient varieties and would have been used by the monks for medical and culinary purposes. We hope that these unusual and personal touches give people the freedom to really experience the abbey ruins and get a truer sense of what it would have been like to live and work in a place of such tranquillity.

BY MAKING AND SELLING a range of freshly made food for twenty five years, using ingredients sourced locally from producers around Yorkshire, we have followed in the footsteps of the monks who originally lived and worked within the abbey's walls. The production of meat, fish, beer, a ewe's milk cheese now recognised as a precursor to today's famous Wensleydale variety, wool, fruit and vegetables would have been the Cistercian monks' livelihood, and essential to keep the community and their home thriving. Each person would have had their own responsibilities that contributed to the overall work, in much the same way that each member of our family has played an integral part in the development of Jervaulx since the Burdon name became intertwined with it in 1971. The future of the abbey depends on the work we do and the honesty of our visitors, a challenge which we've always tried to meet with lots of fresh ideas and commitment from us all. We've been very lucky to share this with our staff, some of whom stayed with us through all three generations. Gayle's husband Alan even found a career in stonemasonry through helping us at the abbey!

In many ways, what our family does at Jervaulx Abbey is a continuation of the original inhabitants' work. This connection to the history of the abbey, and to the generations of our family who have become part of that history, has created, we feel, a unique atmosphere here. Anna, the youngest of the family, sums up the feeling of commitment we all share as a sense of gratitude and privilege: to spend our lifetimes preserving the abbey is as great a contribution as we could ask for, and to have done part of that by indulging our love of home baking and cooking together is something very special indeed. This book is dedicated to all our visitors and to everyone who has enjoyed their time with us at the tearoom. We look forward to remaining at Jervaulx and concentrating our energy and efforts on preserving the future of our beautiful abbey.

Ian, Carol, Gayle and Anna – The Burdon Family

INTRODUCTION

I HAD LONG WANTED TO PRODUCE A RECIPE BOOK, so celebrating twenty five years of baking in the tearoom with our daughters seemed like a perfect opportunity to bring some of our creations together, so that others could enjoy recreating our sweet and savoury delights.

From its opening in 1994, I wanted to base the tearoom on home baking and good food that was locally sourced wherever possible. As time went on it became apparent that there was a need to meet dietary requirements, especially with gluten- and dairy-free cakes, as there was always someone that would miss out on a sweet treat. I developed a range of cakes to meet those needs and took great satisfaction in knowing that all our customers would find that treat awaiting them. Since then, I have also developed a vegan range and some of our favourites have been included in this book. We were very proud to be given the Best Free-From Product award by Deliciously Yorkshire in 2017 for our raspberry and almond cake. The judges' feedback even mentioned that they couldn't tell it was gluten and dairy free! That accolade followed our Best Afternoon Tea award in 2016, so it became apparent then that we were fulfilling my long-term ambitions.

It was to my great joy that when our youngest daughter Anna finished her education in 2010, she was adamant about joining me in the tearoom, and with both of us working together we broadened the scope of the tearoom significantly. Some four years later our eldest daughter Gayle came on board, bringing her talent for sugar craft with her, from which 'Where the Ribbon Ends' was born and began producing bespoke celebration and wedding cakes.

My husband Ian, being a farmer at heart, always liked to lend a hand by producing fruit and vegetables in his garden. He takes great pleasure in popping up to the kitchen with a bucket of produce to challenge us, which was how some of our favourite cakes were created, such as plum crunch and gooseberry and elderflower cake. We never like to waste good food, so even cake crumbs were turned into our Belgian chocolate raspberry truffle cake, a clear winner as far as our customers were concerned. As with many kitchen gardens, there was sometimes a glut of one particular vegetable, so we thought we'd start making our own pickles to go on the tearoom menu. These included Beetroot Relish, Piccalilli, and Wensleydale Beer Chutney, all of which are free from any additives. Our customers loved them and wanted to buy jars to take away, and so began our range of preserves to buy in the tearoom.

Our family still places great emphasis on the ways we can support local food and drink businesses that produce unique ingredients in the county we love. We will maintain these values going forward with our work to preserve the abbey and other, new ventures. We hope that everyone at home is inspired by the recipes in this book to create delicious, homemade cakes and treats, and to celebrate the bounty of the area they live in while enjoying some fantastic food.

Carol Burdon

CLASSICS

These are the recipes that we started out with at the tearoom. They've never gone out of fashion, despite all the changes and trends we have seen over the years, and truly are classic bakes. Some are based on tried and tested flavour combinations, like the blackberry and apple frangipane, and others represent regional specialities such as the Yorkshire curd tart, but all of them are delicious!

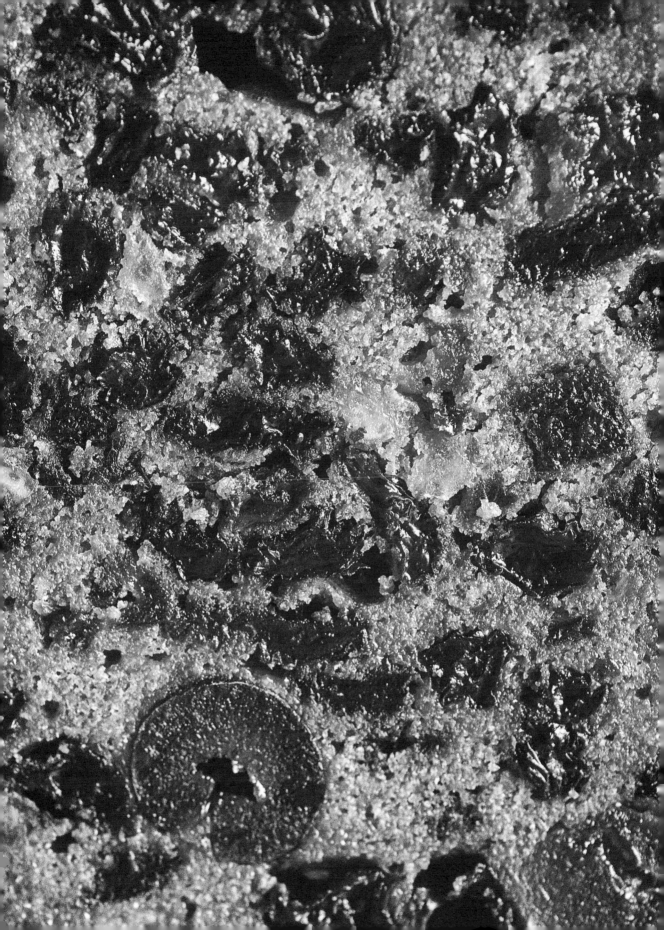

APRICOT AND ORANGE TRAY BAKE

A fresh, light and moist tray bake. This cake is perfect on a warm afternoon with a cuppa.

OVEN TEMPERATURE 170°C/150°C FAN OVEN | 9½X13½ INCH/24X34CM RECTANGULAR CAKE TIN
BAKING TIME 40 MINUTES | SERVES TEN

For the cake:

11oz/312g apricots, chopped

9oz/255g margarine

12oz/340g soft brown sugar

4 eggs

1lb/454g self-raising flour

2 tablespoons orange juice

2 teaspoons orange zest

For the icing:

1lb 4oz/567g icing sugar

2oz/57g butter at room temperature

4 teaspoons orange zest, plus extra for decorating

2-3 tablespoons orange juice

Preheat the oven and line the tin with greaseproof paper.

For the cake

Bring enough water to cover the apricots to the boil in a pan of water, and then add the apricots. Boil for 7-10 minutes or until the apricots are soft. Rinse with cold water and drain well.

Cream together the margarine and sugar, beating on a high speed until the mixture is light and fluffy. Scrape down the sides of the bowl as it's beating to make sure it's fully mixed. Add two of the eggs while mixing on a high power. Reduce the speed, add a little flour and then the remaining two eggs. Slowly increase the speed again and repeat until all of the eggs and flour are mixed.

Add the softened apricots and orange juice and zest and stir in with a wooden spoon. Pour into the tin as soon as possible as the heat from the apricots will start baking the mixture. Bake for approximately 40 minutes, or until a skewer comes out clean. Once the cake has cooled slightly, remove from the tin and then allow to cool completely.

For the icing

Sieve the icing sugar into a small heatproof bowl, then stir in the butter, orange zest and enough orange juice to make a stiff paste. Set over a pan or bowl of hot water and stir until the icing is spreadable. Spread over the top of the cake.

To finish

Sprinkle orange zest over the top of the cake.

APRICOT, ORANGE AND STEM GINGER SYRUP CAKE

This is mum Carol's favourite cake. The recipe has been with us for a long time, and it has such simple and interesting flavours that complement each other perfectly. As the cake is immensely popular with our customers, we always have plenty in the fridge. It also helps to keep Carol sweet!

OVEN TEMPERATURE 170°C/150°C FAN OVEN | 9 INCH/23CM TIN
BAKING TIME 1 HOUR | SERVES TEN

For the cake:
12oz/340g margarine
12oz/340g soft brown sugar
5 eggs
12oz/340g self-raising flour
2 large oranges, zested
2-3 pieces of stem ginger, blended
6oz/170g apricots, chopped

For the syrup:
3 oranges, juiced
6oz/170g caster sugar
3fl oz/85ml water

Preheat the oven and line the base of the cake tin with greaseproof paper.

For the cake

Cream together the margarine and sugar, beating on a high speed until the mixture is light and fluffy. Scrape down the sides of the bowl as its beating to make sure it's fully mixed. Add the eggs, two at a time, on a high power. Reduce the speed and add a little flour in between the eggs, then slowly increase the speed again and repeat until all of the eggs and flour are mixed.

Add the orange zest, ginger and apricots, then beat for a couple of minutes to ensure the mixture is evenly mixed. Pour into the lined cake tin and bake for approximately 1 hour, or until a skewer comes out clean.

For the syrup

While the cake is baking, make the syrup. Place the juice from the oranges into a pan, then add the sugar and water. Bring to a steady boil until the syrup has reduced and becomes slightly thicker. Cover the cake with a layer of the syrup while it's still hot, you may not need to use it all. Leave the cake to cool in the tin.

BLACKBERRY AND APPLE FRANGIPANE

Serve as a pudding or with a cup of tea, hot or cold, it's just as good either way. We used blackberry and apple, but any glut of fruit will be just as good.

OVEN TEMPERATURE 190°C/170°C FAN | 11 INCH/28CM LOOSE-BOTTOMED FLAN TIN
BAKING TIME 35-45 MINUTES | SERVES EIGHT TO TEN

For the pastry:
8oz/227g self-raising flour
4oz/113g margarine
2oz /57g sugar
1 egg

For the filling:
6oz/170g butter or margarine
6oz /170g caster sugar
4 eggs
6oz/170g ground almonds
1 teaspoon almond extract
Enough blackberries to cover the bottom of the pastry case
10oz/270g apple sauce
Icing sugar for dusting

For the pastry

Measure the flour and margarine into a food mixer and pulse until it turns into crumbs. Add the sugar and pulse again for a moment, then add the egg. If the mixture doesn't come together easily, add a tiny splash of cold water. Wrap the pastry in cling film and chill for 30 minutes.

Roll out the pastry on a floured surface and line the flan tin, trimming off any excess that overhangs the sides. Store in the fridge until needed.

For the filling

Cream the butter and the sugar in a mixer until light and fluffy, add the eggs one at a time and blend well before adding the ground almonds and almond extract. Mix well on a low setting.

Fill the pastry case with the blackberries and apple sauce, then top with the almond mixture. Bake for 35 to 45 minutes until the frangipane is golden brown and doesn't wobble. Dust the top with icing sugar just before serving.

BLUE POPPY SEED AND LEMON SYRUP CAKE

This classic lemon cake is an absolute must at the tearoom. The zesty lemon syrup is absolutely loved by everyone who tries it, and we added the poppy seeds to give it a little extra crunch.

OVEN TEMPERATURE 170°C/150°C FAN OVEN | 9 INCH/23CM TIN
BAKING TIME 60-70 MINUTES | SERVES TEN

For the cake:

12oz/340g margarine

12oz/340g caster sugar

5 eggs

12oz/340g self-raising flour

3 lemons, zested

2oz/57g blue poppy seeds

For the syrup:

3 lemons, juiced

6oz/170g caster sugar

3fl oz/85ml water

Preheat the oven and line a tin with greaseproof paper.

For the cake

Cream together the margarine and sugar, beating on a high speed until the mixture is light and fluffy. Scrape down the sides of the bowl as it's beating to make sure it's fully mixed. Add the eggs, two at a time, on a high power. Reduce the speed and add a little flour in between the eggs, then slowly increase the speed again and repeat until all of the eggs and flour are mixed.

Add the lemon zest and poppy seeds, beat for a couple of minutes to ensure it's completely mixed and then pour into the tin. Bake for approximately 1 hour or until a skewer comes out clean.

For the syrup

While the cake is baking, make the syrup. Add the lemon juice, sugar and water to a pan and bring to a steady boil until the syrup has reduced and become slightly thicker. Add the syrup to the cake while it's still hot in the tin, and leave to cool completely before removing from the tin.

Variation

Either leave this as a classic syrup cake or add icing and lemon curd. Slice the cake in half when it's cool, add a layer of vanilla butter icing and a layer of lemon curd. Replace the top half of the cake and add another layer of vanilla icing to the top.

CARROT AND SULTANA CAKE

It's not very often that the first recipe you try is the one you stick with, but we had to make an exception for this stunning carrot cake. It's still one of youngest daughter Anna's absolute favourites. The cake is so soft, the sultanas keep the cake extra moist while adding a delicious sweetness, and it goes perfectly with our cream cheese icing.

OVEN TEMPERATURE 170°C/150°C FAN OVEN | 9½X13½ INCH/24X34CM RECTANGULAR CAKE TIN
BAKING TIME 45 MINUTES | SERVES TEN

4 eggs

12oz/340g soft brown sugar

10fl oz/283ml sunflower oil

8oz/227g plain flour

12oz/340g carrots, grated

2 teaspoons ground cinnamon

2 teaspoons bicarbonate of soda

8oz/227g sultanas

To finish:

Cream cheese icing (recipe on page 120)

Preheat the oven and line the sides and the base of the cake tin. Beat the eggs and sugar together on a high speed until the mixture becomes thick and pale in colour. Continue to beat for a few more minutes before slowly pouring oil into the mixture on a high speed. Reduce the speed and fold in all of the dry ingredients until they're evenly distributed. Pour the mixture into the cake tin and bake for 45 minutes or until a skewer comes out clean. A crust may have formed on top of the cake that may trick you into thinking it's baked so check before you take it out of the oven.

To finish

Once the cake has completely cooled, add the cream cheese icing.

DOUBLE CHOCOLATE CHEESECAKE

This recipe is one of youngest daughter Anna's favourites. The delicious pairing of the creamy white chocolate and the smooth milk chocolate ganache means this irresistibly rich cheesecake is always a firm favourite at the tearoom.

OVEN TEMPERATURE 180°C/160°C FAN OVEN | 9½X13½ INCH/24X34CM RECTANGULAR CAKE TIN
BAKING TIME 45-50 MINUTES | SERVES TEN

For the biscuit base:

7oz/198g margarine

1lb/454g biscuit crumbs

For the white chocolate centre:

1lb 8oz/680g cream cheese

8oz/227g caster sugar

6 eggs

10oz/283g white chocolate, melted

For the ganache topping:

10oz/283g Belgian milk chocolate

11fl oz/312ml cream

Preheat the oven and line both the sides and the base of the cake tin.

For the biscuit base

Gently melt the margarine in a pan and add the biscuit crumbs, then mix until completely combined. Press into the base of the tin, spreading evenly.

For the white chocolate centre

With a hand mixer, cream together the cream cheese and sugar. Add one egg at a time, making sure each egg is fully mixed in before adding the next. Melt the white chocolate and add it to the mixture, mixing on a medium speed. Make sure there are no lumps.

Pour the filling over the pressed biscuit base and bake the cheesecake in the centre of the oven for 45 to 50 minutes until the top has started to brown slightly. There should still be a slight wobble in the centre with the outside nice and firm. Remove from the oven and allow to cool completely before adding the ganache topping.

For the ganache topping

Place the Belgian chocolate and cream into a bowl over a pan of hot water and allow to melt, stirring constantly to make sure it doesn't burn. Pour the ganache onto the chilled cheesecake and pop it into the fridge until cooled.

FRUITY TEA BREAD

We love the versatility of this tea bread as it can be changed to suit whatever mood you're in. You can enjoy it with some (or a lot of!) butter, or even the traditional Yorkshire accompaniment of Wensleydale cheese. It's superbly simple to make, and even easier to eat.

OVEN TEMPERATURE 170°C/150°C FAN OVEN | 1LB LOAF TIN
BAKING TIME 1 HOUR | SERVES EIGHT

6oz/170g raisins
6oz/170g dates, chopped
2oz/57g figs
2oz/57g prunes, destoned
1 mug of berry-flavoured tea
1 orange, zested
8oz/227g soft brown sugar
8oz/227g self-raising flour
1 egg, beaten

Preheat the oven and line the cake tin with greaseproof paper. Soak the dried fruit in a large glass bowl overnight in the hot tea. Once soaked, add the rest of the ingredients to the bowl and mix by hand until the egg is evenly combined and no flour is surrounding the fruit. Pour the mixture into the prepared tin, using a knife to make sure the top is evenly flat. Bake for approximately 1 hour, or until a skewer comes out clean. Leave to cool in the tin completely before removing.

Variations

The flavours in this tea bread can be as diverse as you like; simple changes can create a whole new taste. Different fruit teas are an easy way to do this. Our favourites are berry-flavoured teas as used above. You can also swap the figs and prunes for any of your favourites fruits, as long as you keep the weight the same. For example, you could use cranberries or apricots as an alternative.

LEMONY TREACLE TART

This tart is not only a real treat with a cup of tea in the afternoon, it doubles up as a pudding after Sunday lunch served warm with ice cream.

OVEN TEMPERATURE 180°C/160°C FAN | 9 INCH/23CM LOOSE-BOTTOMED TART TIN
BAKING TIME 30-35 MINUTES | SERVES EIGHT

For the pastry:
6oz/170g self-raising flour
Pinch of salt
3oz/85g cold margarine
1 large egg, beaten
Cold water (if needed)

For the filling:
1lb 12oz/794g golden syrup
4½oz/125g breadcrumbs
1½ lemons, zested
2oz/57g rolled oats
2 large eggs, whisked

For the pastry

Put the flour, salt and margarine in a large bowl and rub together until the mixture resembles breadcrumbs. Add the egg gradually while combining until you have a firm dough. If the mixture doesn't come together easily, add a tiny splash of cold water. Wrap in cling film and chill for 30 minutes. Roll out the pastry and line the tart tin, trimming off any excess that overhangs the sides. Store in the fridge until needed.

For the filling

Warm the syrup in a pan, ensuring that it doesn't boil, and then stir in the breadcrumbs, lemon zest, oats and eggs. Pour into the pastry case and bake the treacle tart in the preheated oven for 30 to 35 minutes. The filling may still be slightly wobbly after this time but it will set as it cools. Leave in the tin to cool before turning out.

PEAR, HAZELNUT AND CHOCOLATE CAKE

Chocolate and hazelnut is a time-honoured combination, but adding fresh pear brings a whole new fruity dimension to this cake. The pears add moisture and also give the cake the perfect balance of sweetness and nuttiness. Most importantly though, it's still rich and chocolatey.

OVEN TEMPERATURE 170°C/150°C FAN OVEN | 9 INCH/23CM TIN
BAKING TIME 30-35 MINUTES | SERVES TWELVE | BAKE TWO FOR A TWO TIERED VERSION AS SHOWN

5 small ripe pears

3oz/85g hazelnuts, blanched

5oz/142g self-raising flour

6oz/170g margarine

2 eggs

5oz/142g caster sugar

2oz/57g dark chocolate, chopped into small chunks

To finish:

Chocolate icing (recipe on page 120)

Bake this recipe twice to create the cake photographed.

Preheat the oven and line the base of the cake tin with greaseproof paper.

Peel and core two pears, cut into small cubes and then set aside. Do the same with the other three and set to one side, separately from the first two. In a food processor, blend the hazelnuts to a fine consistency, stopping before they turn to powder. Mix the flour with the hazelnuts, then add the margarine, pulsing until a crumb-like mixture forms. Pour the crumb mixture into a mixing bowl, then add the eggs and sugar and mix well on a medium speed. Add the two pears and the dark chocolate before pouring the mixture into the prepared cake tin. Scatter the remaining pear on top, pressing the cubes slightly into the mixture to avoid burning. Bake for 30 to 35 minutes or until a skewer comes out clean.

How to blanch hazelnuts

Hazelnuts with their skin left on can be quite bitter, so blanching them achieves the nicest results.

Heat 32fl oz/900ml of water in a large saucepan and bring to the boil. Once boiling, add four tablespoons of bicarbonate of soda and 9oz/255g of hazelnuts. Boil the hazelnuts for 3 minutes, scooping off any foam that may form from the bubbling.

After 3 minutes, test a hazelnut by removing it from the pan and placing it under cold water. If the skin comes off easily, they are ready. If not, allow another 15 seconds and try again. Repeat until the skin comes away easily. Drain the nuts and rinse well under cold water. Dry with a paper towel.

RICH FRUIT CAKE

This is a moist rich fruit cake that does not need to mature. You can mix the fruits according to your personal preference; we leave out the currants and add more sultanas and raisins. Other dried fruits such as cranberries or blueberries can be added, and if you don't like or can't have almonds just add the same amount of an ingredient you do like.

OVEN TEMPERATURE 140°C/120°C FAN OVEN | 9 INCH/23CM LOOSE-BOTTOMED TIN
BAKING TIME APPROXIMATELY 6 HOURS

1lb 12oz/794g currants

13oz/369g each of sultanas and raisins

5oz/142g mixed peel

9oz/255g glacé cherries

5oz/142g flaked almonds

1lb 5oz/595g plain flour

1 teaspoon each of mixed spice and cinnamon

1lb 2oz/510g each of softened butter and brown sugar

½ lemon, zested

9 medium-sized eggs, beaten

2-3 tablespoons brandy or whiskey

Preheat the oven and line the cake tin with a double layer of baking parchment.

In a very large bowl or a clean bucket, mix all the dried fruit and peel, chop the cherries in half if desired (we like to keep them whole) and add the flaked almonds if using. Sift the flour and spices into the same bowl or bucket and mix well to cover all the fruit. Adding the flour at this stage prevents the fruit from sinking to the bottom when the cake is baking.

Put the butter, sugar and lemon zest into a separate bowl and cream together until pale and fluffy; this should take about 5 minutes. Add the eggs one at a time, beating well before adding the next egg. You may find the mixture curdles towards the end, but don't worry if this does happen.

Add the creamed mixture to the fruit mixture; the best way to combine them is to get your hands in and mix well until all the flour has been absorbed into the batter. Transfer the mixture into the prepared tin, spreading it evenly and making sure there are no air pockets. Make a hollow in the centre to ensure the cake comes out with an even surface when baked.

Wrap a double layer of brown paper around the outside of the tin and secure with string. Bake until a skewer comes out clean, checking the cake from time to time. Cover with brown paper if the top is browning too quickly.

When cooked, leave the fruit cake to cool in the tin before turning out onto a cooling rack, prick the top with a fine skewer and slowly pour the brandy or whiskey over it. Wrap the cake in a double layer of parchment and place in an airtight tin.

STICKY ORANGE FLAPJACK

This is eldest daughter Gayle's favourite recipe. She used to make this all the time when she was younger. Gayle always made it with margarine instead of butter because she preferred the taste, so have a play around and see which you like best.

OVEN TEMPERATURE 190°C/170°C FAN OVEN | 9½X13½ INCH/24X34CM RECTANGULAR CAKE TIN
BAKING TIME 35-40 MINUTES | SERVES SIXTEEN

18oz/510g margarine
18oz/510g caster sugar
18oz/510g golden syrup
30oz/850g jumbo oats
3 oranges, zested
4 tablespoons marmalade

Line the sides and the base of the baking tray with greaseproof paper and preheat the oven.

Place the margarine, sugar and syrup into a pan and stir over a gentle heat. When melted, remove from the heat and add the oats and orange zest, stirring until evenly mixed.

Bake for 35 to 40 minutes. The outside may turn golden brown, but make sure the centre doesn't wobble. Once baked, remove from the oven.

In a bowl, add one tablespoon of water to the marmalade. Warm the mixture and spread over the top of the baked flapjack.

Hints and tips

Don't have your oven too high, as it will burn the outside and make the flapjack very tough. If the flapjack cools in the fridge it will become quite firm.

SWEET MINCEMEAT CRUMBLE TART

This tart is not only great for Christmas, it's a good all-rounder throughout the year. For example, swapping the mincemeat for rhubarb and plum transforms this tart into an amazing summertime treat.

OVEN TEMPERATURE 180°C/160°C FAN | 9 INCH/23CM LOOSE-BOTTOMED TIN
BAKING TIME 30-35 MINUTES | SERVES EIGHT TO TEN

For the pastry:
6oz/170g self-raising flour
3oz/85g cold margarine
Pinch of salt
1 large egg

For the filling:
14oz/397g mincemeat
9oz/255g Bramley apple sauce

For the crumble:
3½oz/100g plain flour
2½oz/75g butter
2oz/57g rolled oats
3½oz/100g Demerara sugar

For the pastry

Blend the flour and butter with a pinch of salt in a food processor for a few seconds until the mixture looks like breadcrumbs. Add the egg and combine until the mixture comes together to form a firm dough. Wrap in cling film and chill for 30 minutes.

For the filling

Roll out the pastry and line the tin, gently pressing into the corners and trimming the overhang with a sharp knife. Fill the pastry case with the mincemeat and apple sauce and then store in the fridge until needed.

For the crumble

Blend the flour and butter in a food processor for a few seconds, until the mixture looks like breadcrumbs. Stir in the oats and the brown sugar then sprinkle the crumble over the filling. Bake the tart in the oven for 30 to 35 minutes, or until crisp and golden brown on top.

To serve

Once cool enough to handle, you can turn out the tart and serve it warm with ice cream or custard, although it's just as good cold with a cuppa the next day.

TRADITIONAL FRUIT SCONE

This delightfully traditional scone was an absolute must for this recipe book. Our cream teas are one of the biggest sellers in the tearoom, as our scones are perfect for breakfast, elevenses, a light lunch or an afternoon treat. There's no wrong time to treat yourself to one, especially with the inviting addition of a cinnamon topping.

OVEN TEMPERATURE 200°C/180°C FAN OVEN | FLAT BAKING TRAY
BAKING TIME 20 MINUTES | MAKES SIXTEEN

1lb/454g self-raising flour

8oz/227g margarine

4oz/113g caster sugar

3 eggs

14fl oz/397ml milk

6oz/170g mixed dried fruit

For the topping

1 egg, beaten

Sprinkle of Demerara sugar and ground cinnamon

Preheat the oven.

In the bowl of an electric mixer, thoroughly combine the flour, margarine and sugar on a medium speed. Crack the eggs into a measuring jug and add the milk up to ¾ pint, whisking until blended. Pour the egg mixture into the flour, mixing on a medium speed until all the liquid has been added. Reduce the speed and add the fruit, until the mixture comes together. Be careful not to overmix as this will beat the air out.

Flour the work surface and place the scone mixture on top, being careful not to over-handle the mixture. Roll out the dough mix to the same height at your cutter (we use a cutter 3cm high and 7cm wide). Cut out your scones and place onto a greased baking tray, then glaze the top of each one with the beaten egg and add a sprinkle of Demerara sugar and ground cinnamon.

Bake for about 10 minutes, then turn the tray around and bake for another 10 minutes until the tops are golden brown and a hollow sound is made when the base of the scone is tapped.

Allow to cool and enjoy with a nice hot cup of tea.

TUNISIAN ORANGE CAKE

We've been making this cake for years, but after rereading the original recipe recently, we discovered we'd been making it wrong! After testing the original recipe properly, we actually preferred our way of making it, which creates a very moist and sweet cake.

OVEN TEMPERATURE 170˚C/150˚C FAN OVEN | 9 INCH/23CM TIN (AVOID LOOSE-BOTTOMED TINS AS THE MIXTURE IS VERY WET) | BAKING TIME 45-50 MINUTES | SERVES NINE

For the cake:

2oz/57g breadcrumbs

7oz/198g caster sugar

3oz/85g ground almonds

1½ teaspoons baking powder

1 orange, zested

½ lemon, zested

7fl oz/198ml sunflower oil

4 eggs

For the syrup:

2 oranges, juiced

1 lemon, juiced

3fl oz/85ml water

6oz/170g caster sugar

Line the base of the tin with greaseproof paper and preheat the oven.

For the cake

Add all of the dry ingredients and zest into a mixing bowl, then add the oil and eggs and mix on a medium speed until all of the dry ingredients are blended. The mixture will be very runny.

Pour the mixture into the prepared tin and bake for 45 to 50 minutes, or until a skewer comes out clean. A crust will form over the cake which might trick you into thinking it's baked before it's actually done. Don't expect this cake to rise much.

For the syrup

While the cake is cooking, make the syrup. Place all of the ingredients into a pan and bring to the boil, letting it thicken slightly. Add as much syrup as you want to the cake while they're both still hot and the cake is still in the tin. Wait until the cake is completely cool before removing it from the tin.

UPSTAIRS DOWNSTAIRS SHORTBREAD

There is always a family recipe that gets passed down through the generations; here is ours. Ian's mother, Jean Burdon, was brought up with this recipe. Nanny, as we knew her, saw the need to offer refreshments for visitors to Jervaulx Abbey from a small caravan where she made tea and coffee. Another of Nanny's passions was her rose garden, so after she passed in 2015 we rescued all her beloved roses and replanted them at the tearoom. Today a beautiful rose garden stands at the gates in her memory.

OVEN TEMPERATURE 170°C/150°C FAN OVEN | BAKING TRAY
BAKING TIME 20 MINUTES | SERVES SIXTEEN

4oz/113g caster sugar

8oz/227g butter, slightly colder than room temperature

12oz/340g plain flour

Pinch of salt

Preheat the oven.

Beat the sugar and butter until blended and lighter in colour. Stir in the flour and pinch of salt.

Sprinkle a light covering of flour onto a clean flat surface. Lightly cover the rolling pin with flour and roll out the mixture to around 1cm in height, then use a 7cm wide round cutter to cut out each piece. Carefully transfer the shortbread rounds to the baking tray and then place in the preheated oven.

Bake for 10 minutes and then check on the shortbread. Turn the baking tray round and bake for a further 10 minutes. It should be slightly coloured, so bake for a few more minutes if needed.

Once baked, add a sugar topping to your shortbread. Caster sugar was traditionally used, but Demerara sugar will add more of a crunch.

WENSLEYDALE CHEESE AND SESAME SEED SCONES

Our cheese scones are a massively popular choice, especially when you're craving a light, savoury snack. When this is paired with our Wensleydale beer chutney, you get a great combination of Wensleydale's finest. If Wensleydale isn't your cup of tea though, you can easily switch this for any cheese of your choice.

OVEN TEMPERATURE 200°C/180°C FAN OVEN | FLAT BAKING TRAY
BAKING TIME 20-25 MINUTES | MAKES SIX

12oz/340g self-raising flour

2oz/57g margarine

6oz/170g Wensleydale cheese, grated

½ teaspoons mixed herbs

2 eggs

2fl oz/57ml milk

For the topping:

1 egg, beaten

Extra grated cheese

A sprinkle of sesame seeds

Preheat the oven.

Place the flour, margarine, grated cheese and mixed herbs in a mixing bowl and mix on a medium-slow speed until evenly blended. In a jug, whisk together the eggs and milk until completely combined. Pour the egg mixture into the flour bowl, and mix on a medium speed until all the liquid has been added. Reduce the speed and continue until the mixture comes together. Be careful not to overmix and beat the air out.

Flour the work surface and remove the dough from the bowl, being careful not to over-handle the mixture. Roll out to the same height as a 3cm deep by 7.5cm wide round cutter, cut out your scones and place them onto the baking tray.

For the topping

Glaze the scones with the beaten egg and add a sprinkle of grated cheese and sesame seeds on the top. Bake for about 10 minutes, then turn the tray around and bake for another 10 minutes until the tops are golden brown and a hollow sound is made when the base of the scone is tapped.

WENSLEYDALE, GINGER AND APRICOT CHEESECAKE

This delicious cheesecake is a welcome taste of the Yorkshire Dales. This recipe has been with us for over twenty years; it's really easy to make and gives such a lovely flavour. It's perfect on its own, or you can serve it with cream for a real indulgence.

9 INCH/23CM TIN | CHILLING TIME OVERNIGHT | SERVES TEN

For the base:

6oz/170g margarine

1lb/454g biscuits, crumbed

For the cheesecake:

12oz/340g full-fat cream cheese

2oz/57g sugar

12oz/340g Wensleydale cheese, grated

3oz/85g apricots, chopped

2 pieces of stem ginger, blended

4 tablespoons cream

Line the base of the cake tin with greaseproof paper.

For the base

Gently melt the margarine, then add the biscuit crumbs and mix with a wooden spoon. Pour into the base of the tin and press down to create a firm base.

For the cheesecake

In a mixing bowl, add the cream cheese and beat well. Add the Wensleydale cheese, apricots and ginger. Mix well and add one tablespoon of cream at a time. When it's completely mixed, pour into the tin and press the mixture firmly down with a spatula. Chill overnight in the fridge.

YORKSHIRE CURD TART

Curds are difficult to find in shops, so we use cream cheese in this recipe making it seriously, deliciously creamy!

OVEN TEMPERATURE 200°C/180°C FAN | 9 INCH/23CM LOOSE-BOTTOMED TIN
BAKING TIME 55 MINUTES | SERVES TEN

For the pastry:
7oz/198g plain flour
3½oz/100g butter, cubed
1oz/28g caster sugar
2-3 tablespoons cold water

For the filling:
3oz/85g butter, softened
3oz/85g caster sugar
1lb 2oz/510g full-fat cream cheese
1 lemon, zested and juiced
3 eggs, beaten
2oz/57g sultanas
Freshly ground nutmeg
Icing sugar, for dusting

Preheat the oven, then grease the tart tin and place it on a flat baking tray.

For the pastry

Put the flour in an electric mixer or food processor, add the butter and put on a low speed until the mixture resembles breadcrumbs. Stir in the sugar then gradually add two to three tablespoons of very cold water and combine until you have a firm dough. Wrap the pastry in cling film and leave to rest in the fridge for 30 minutes. Roll out the chilled pastry to an 11 inch/28cm round and ease it into the bottom of the prepared tin. Cover the pastry with greaseproof paper, fill with baking beans or rice and blind bake for 15 minutes, then remove the beans or rice and greaseproof paper and bake for a further 5 minutes. Take out and reduce the oven temperature to 180°C/160°C fan.

For the filling

Beat the butter and sugar for 5 minutes in an electric mixer until pale and light. Stir in the cream cheese and lemon zest until well blended. Gradually beat in the lemon juice followed by the eggs, a little at a time. Stir in the sultanas, then pour the mixture into the pastry case and bake for 30 to 35 minutes until the filling is set about 2 inches in from the edge and pale golden on the surface (it will set completely as it cools). Cool in the tin for about 10 minutes before transferring to a plate. Sprinkle with nutmeg and icing sugar, and serve warm or cold.

NEWBIES

Baking has moved with the times, and much as we all love the classics of our parents' and grandparents' generation, it's good to embrace change. New styles of decoration and flavours have been introduced to everyone through social media and a new generation of creative, inventive bakers. We've followed suit with our own additions and twists on old favourites, like the millionaire's cake, which are among our most popular tearoom treats.

BANANA CAKE

A few years ago, eldest daughter Gayle had her first request for a banana wedding cake through Where The Ribbon Ends, her bespoke celebration cake business. The cake of course needed to have an even bake, and most importantly, taste amazing. After more than a week of trialling and tweaking different recipes, this one is our absolute favourite.

OVEN TEMPERATURE 170°C/150°C FAN OVEN | 9 INCH/23CM TIN OR 1LB LOAF TIN
BAKING TIME 1 HOUR 10 MINUTES | SERVES TEN

10oz/283g margarine
10oz/283g caster sugar
4 eggs
10oz/283g self-raising flour
1 teaspoon baking powder
2 small ripe bananas, mashed

Preheat the oven and line the cake tin.

Cream together the margarine and sugar, beating on a high speed until the mixture is light and fluffy. Scrape down the sides of the bowl as its beating to make sure it's fully mixed. Add the eggs, two at a time, on a high power. Reduce the speed and add a little flour in between the eggs, then slowly increase the speed again and repeat until all of the eggs, flour and baking powder are mixed.

Finally, add the mashed bananas to the mixture and beat for a couple of minutes to ensure that the mixture is completely combined before pouring into the tin. Bake for 1 hour 10 minutes, either using a loaf tin or 9 inch round tin, until a skewer comes out clean. Leave to cool completely before removing from the tin.

To finish

The cake is delicious as it is but by adding honey to the top whilst the cake is still warm, it's a perfect way to add that little something extra.

Variations

For a banoffee cake, slice through the middle of the cake and add a layer of caramel sauce and a layer of cream cheese icing. Replace the top half of the cake and add a layer of cream cheese icing to the top and the sides of the cake. Finish with a drizzle of caramel sauce.

Add fresh raspberries, sliced banana and cream cheese icing for a light, summery cake. Slice the middle of the cake, and add a layer of cream cheese icing to the bottom half. Place fresh raspberries and fresh sliced banana on the icing, adding extra cream cheese icing to cover the fruit. Replace the top half of the cake and add a layer of icing on top. Smooth over and decorate with fresh raspberries and slices of banana.

CARROT AND COCONUT CAKE

This carrot cake is often used for wedding cakes with Where The Ribbon Ends; the coconut adds a great texture while the sultanas retain moisture. With a delicious crunchy finish, matched with soft sweet icing, it becomes irresistible.

OVEN TEMPERATURE 170°C/150°C FAN OVEN | 9 INCH/23CM TIN
BAKING TIME 1 HOUR 30 MINUTES | SERVES TEN

4 eggs

14oz/397g soft brown sugar

10fl oz/283ml sunflower oil

14oz/397g plain flour

3½oz/100g desiccated coconut

5oz/142g pineapple, diced (optional)

14oz/397g carrots, grated

2 teaspoons ground cinnamon

2 teaspoons bicarbonate of soda

7oz/198g sultanas

To finish:

Cream cheese icing (recipe on page 120)

or

Vanilla icing (recipe on page 116)

Preheat the oven and line the sides and the base of the cake tin.

Beat the eggs and sugar together on a high speed until the mixture becomes thick and pale in colour. Continue to beat for a few more minutes before slowly pouring oil with a steady stream into the mixture on a high speed. The mixture should hold the shape of the trail.

Reduce to a slow speed to add all of the dry ingredients until they're evenly distributed. Stir in the pineapple by hand if you want to include it, do not add sultanas.

Pour the mixture into the cake tin and bake for 1 hour 30 minutes or until a skewer comes out clean.

To finish

Once the cake has completely cooled, slice the cake through the middle and add the cream cheese icing or vanilla icing.

CHOCOLATE BANANA CAKE

This gorgeous cake has the perfect pairing of banana and chocolate, and its moistness means that it lasts for a good few days. A perfect treat throughout the week.

OVEN TEMPERATURE 170°C/150°C FAN OVEN | 9 INCH/23CM TIN
BAKING TIME 1 HOUR | SERVES TEN

7oz/198g Belgian chocolate

11oz/312g margarine

12oz/340g caster sugar

6 eggs

12oz/340g self-raising flour

2 teaspoons baking powder

2oz/57g cocoa powder

2 ripe bananas, mashed

To finish:

Chocolate icing (recipe on page 120)

Line the cake tin and preheat the oven.

Melt the chocolate in a bowl over a pan of hot water and leave to one side.

Cream together the margarine and sugar until light and fluffy, then gradually add the eggs one at a time. Scrape around the bowl and add a little flour after each egg to avoid splitting.

Sift the flour, baking powder and cocoa powder into the mixture, and finally add the melted chocolate and mashed bananas. Mix well before pouring into the tin. Bake for 1 hour or until a skewer comes out clean.

To finish

If you want something a little fancier, pour chocolate ganache over the cake while it's still in the tin, leaving to cool completely before removing. See page 121 for the ganache recipe.

CHUBBY SCOUNDRELS

Are they cakes? Are they scones? We think they're the best of both worlds. Perfect split in half and spread with butter, this is one of dad Ian's favourite bakes, so we're dedicating this recipe to him.

OVEN TEMPERATURE 170°C/150°C FAN OVEN | 9½X13½ INCH/24X34CM RECTANGULAR CAKE TIN
BAKING TIME 20-25 MINUTES | SERVES TEN

5oz/142g plain flour
5oz/142g self-raising flour
1 teaspoon baking powder
4oz/113g butter, chilled
3oz/85g caster sugar
1 orange, zested
1 lemon, zested
1 teaspoon cinnamon
½ teaspoon nutmeg
5oz/142g dried mixed fruit
1 egg
2fl oz/57ml milk

For the topping:
1 egg, beaten
Flaked almonds
Glacé cherries
Demerara sugar

Preheat the oven.

Add both the flours with the baking powder into a mixing bowl and combine. Cut the cold butter in cubes, add to the mixing bowl and gently crumble with your fingertips until a breadcrumb-like texture is achieved. Add the sugar, both zests, cinnamon, nutmeg, and fruit and mix well. Add the egg and the milk to bind the mixture from crumbs to a dough.

Bring the mixture together into a ball and then divide into six smaller balls. Roll them in the palm of your hand to make them an even shape, place onto your baking tray and flatten slightly. Brush the tops with the beaten egg, and add any or all of the flaked almonds, glacé cherries and a sprinkle of Demerara sugar to finish.

Bake for 20-25 minutes until they are golden brown and sound hollow when the base is tapped.

GINGER BEER CAKE

This is such a great twist on a chocolate cake, it's perfect to impress your friends and family. Using actual ginger beer adds extra moisture to this irresistible cake.

OVEN TEMPERATURE 170°C/150°C FAN OVEN | 9 INCH/23CM TIN (AVOID LOOSE-BOTTOMED TINS AS THE MIXTURE IS VERY WET) | BAKING TIME 1 HOUR | SERVES TWELVE

9oz/255g margarine

8fl oz/227g ginger beer

14oz/397g caster sugar

3oz/85g cocoa powder

2 eggs

5fl oz/142ml milk

1 teaspoon ground ginger

10oz/283g plain flour

2 teaspoons bicarbonate of soda

½ teaspoon baking powder

To finish:

Chocolate icing (recipe on page 120)

Preheat the oven and line the base of the tin with greaseproof paper. In a saucepan, gently melt the margarine in the ginger beer. Remove the pan from the heat and using a hand whisk, mix in the sugar and cocoa powder. Increase the speed of the hand whisk and mix in the eggs and milk.

In a separate bowl, add all of the dry ingredients and pour into the warm chocolate mixture, mixing together on a slower speed. Once there are no lumps, pour into the prepared cake tin and bake for 1 hour, or until a skewer comes out clean. Allow to cool.

To finish

Slice the cake in half and spread a thick layer of chocolate icing over the bottom half of the cake. Replace the top half of the cake and add more icing to the top. With a spatula, spread a thick amount of icing on to cover the whole cake.

To get the effect pictured, place the cake on a turntable and use a small-bladed spatula. Starting from the bottom to get a straight first line, apply a slight pressure to the icing with the tip of the spatula. Keeping the pressure even and your hand still, turn the table with your other hand until you complete the circle. Continue until you reach the top of the cake. Use the same technique to decorate the top of the cake. Practice makes perfect!

GINGER SYRUP CAKE WITH A BISCUIT BASE

A twist on a golden oldie. This sweet and sticky cake was always a firm favourite at events at our tearoom. The biscuit base gives it a definite crunch, and the syrup really adds a kick of sweet ginger, leaving you with a winning combination of taste and texture.

OVEN TEMP 170°C/150°C FAN OVEN | 9 INCH/23CM TIN
BAKING TIME 50 MINUTES | SERVES NINE

For the biscuit base:

4oz/113g margarine

10oz/283g biscuit crumbs

For the cake:

3oz/85g margarine

6 tablespoons golden syrup

4oz/113g Demerara sugar

½ egg

5fl oz/142ml milk

8oz/227g plain flour

1½ teaspoons ground ginger

1½ teaspoons baking powder

½ teaspoon bicarbonate soda

For the syrup:

6oz/170g caster sugar

6fl oz/170ml water

1½ teaspoons ground ginger

Preheat the oven and line the cake tin with greaseproof paper.

For the biscuit base

Melt the margarine in a pan over a low heat, being careful not to burn it. Add the biscuit crumbs and mix together until completely combined. Pour into the base of the tin and press down until it's firm.

For the cake

Place the margarine, syrup and sugar into a pan and heat until melted, but do not boil. If the mixture gets too hot, leave to cool a little before continuing, or the egg will start to cook. Slowly add the egg and milk to the mixture, and whisk with a hand mixer.

Slowly add the dry ingredients while whisking, making sure no lumps are formed. When the mixture is like a batter, pour into the prepared tin. Bake for approximately 50 minutes or until a skewer comes out clean. Add the syrup while the cake is still hot, then leave to cool completely in the tin.

For the syrup

Place the ingredients into a pan and bring to the boil, then reduce the mixture down to a syrup. The syrup should thicken slightly but still be thin enough to pour over the hot cake.

GOOSEBERRY AND ELDERFLOWER CAKE

After a pretty good season for gooseberries, dad Ian brought us a big bucket of them, which inspired this light and sweet cake. Perfect in summer!

OVEN TEMPERATURE 170°C/150°C FAN OVEN | 9 INCH/23CM TIN
BAKING TIME 1 HOUR 10 MINUTES, OR UNTIL A SKEWER COMES OUT CLEAN | SERVES TEN

For the cake:

12oz/340g margarine

12oz/340g caster sugar

5 eggs

12oz/340g self-raising flour

3 tablespoons elderflower cordial, plus extra for icing

9oz/255g gooseberries, topped and tailed

For the icing:

Butter icing (recipe on page 120)

Fresh elderflower and mint leaves

Preheat the oven and line the base of the cake tin with greaseproof paper.

For the cake

Cream together the margarine and sugar, beating on a high speed until the mixture is light and fluffy. Scrape down the sides of the bowl as it's beating to make sure it's fully mixed. Stir in the elderflower cordial, and then add the eggs, two at a time, on a high speed. Reduce the speed and add a little flour in between each addition of egg, then slowly increase the speed again and repeat until all of the eggs and flour are mixed. Stir in the gooseberries by hand, and then pour the mixture into the lined cake tin and bake for approximately 1 hour 10 minutes, or until a skewer comes out clean.

For the icing

Using the butter icing recipe from finishing touches, add a little elderflower cordial to the butter icing and mix well. Slice the cake in half through the middle and cover the bottom with a layer of icing. Replace the top and cover the whole cake with icing. Using a small spatula, apply a small amount of pressure to the base and then move the spatula upwards to smooth out the icing. Continue around the cake to complete the finish and then decorate with fresh elderflower and mint.

MILLIONAIRE'S CAKE

The thought behind this cake was simple: let's take the famous millionaire's shortbread and make it into a cake! The result was three layers of pure deliciousness.

OVEN TEMPERATURE 170°C/150°C FAN OVEN | 9 INCH/23CM TIN
BAKING TIME 1 HOUR 15 MINUTES | SERVES TWELVE

For the biscuit base:

4oz/113g margarine

10oz/283g biscuit crumbs

For the caramel cake:

12oz/340g margarine

12oz/340g soft brown sugar

5 eggs

12oz/340g self-raising flour

1 tablespoon caramel sauce (recipe on page 122)

To finish:

Chocolate icing (recipe on page 120)

Chocolate ganache (recipe on page 121)

Preheat the oven and line the cake tin with greaseproof paper.

For the biscuit base

Melt the margarine in a pan over a low heat, being careful not to burn it. Add the biscuit crumbs and mix together until completely combined. Place into the base of the cake tin and press down firmly.

For the caramel cake

Cream together the margarine and sugar, beating on a high speed until the mixture is light and fluffy. Scrape down the sides of the bowl as it's beating to make sure it's fully mixed. Add the eggs, two at a time, on a high power. Reduce the speed and add a little flour in between the eggs, then slowly increase the speed again and repeat until all of the eggs and flour are mixed. Add the caramel sauce and beat for a couple of minutes to make sure it's thoroughly mixed. Pour into the cake tin and bake for approximately 1 hour 15 minutes, or until a skewer comes out clean. Leave the cake to cool slightly in the tin, then remove and allow to cool completely.

To finish

Slice the cake layer evenly across to get two rounds, not including the biscuit base or the top layer will be too thick. Spread a layer of chocolate icing on the bottom layer of the cake, then put the top layer back on. Using a palette knife smooth the chocolate ganache over the top of the cake. We have used salted caramel to create the drip look, as pictured.

NANA BELL'S FLAPJACK

The most amazing flapjack we've ever had was made by Gayle and Annas best friend's mum Isobel, who was kind enough to give us the recipe. Now a grandmother, which is how Isobel gained her new name Nana Bell, this recipe is dedicated to the whole Riley family.

OVEN TEMPERATURE 190°C/170°C FAN OVEN | 9½X13½ INCH/24X34CM RECTANGULAR CAKE TIN
BAKING TIME 30 MINUTES | SERVES SIXTEEN

1lb/454g butter
6oz/170g Demerara sugar
6oz/170g soft brown sugar
12oz/340g golden syrup
1lb 10oz/737g jumbo oats

White chocolate ganache:

10oz/283g white chocolate
7fl oz/198ml cream

Preheat the oven and line both the sides and the base of the baking tray with greaseproof paper.

Melt the butter, sugar and syrup in a pan over a gentle heat, stirring often. Once melted, remove from the heat and add the oats. Stir until the oats are evenly covered, then pour into the tin and press down firmly with a spatula.

Bake for 30 minutes or until the top is golden and the centre doesn't wobble. Allow to cool for a few minutes, then press down again with a spatula.

Hints and tips

Don't have your oven too high or it will burn the outside of the flapjack, making it very tough. A nice golden brown colour is ideal but it's crucial that the centre doesn't wobble.

Variations

For a white chocolate and raspberry flapjack, spread half of the oat mixture into the tin, add a generous helping of frozen raspberries and cover with the rest of the mixture. Add a white chocolate ganache to the top when the flapjack is cooked and cooled.

For the white chocolate ganache

Over a pan of hot water, in a bowl, melt both the chocolate and cream. Stir until all chocolate has melted. Pour over the top of the cooled flapjack.

PLUM CRUNCH

Perfect in the summer for a light afternoon treat. The crunchy sugary topping of this cake really complements the tartness of the plums. This recipe was inspired by a glut of fresh Victoria plums from the garden.

OVEN TEMPERATURE 170°C/150°C FAN OVEN | 1LB LOAF TIN
BAKING TIME 45-50 MINUTES | SERVES EIGHT

For the cake:

10oz/283g (usually 3) fresh plums

7oz/198g margarine

7oz/198g caster sugar

3 eggs

7oz/198g self-raising flour

1½ teaspoons vanilla extract

3 tablespoons milk

1½ teaspoons baking powder

For the crunch topping:

2 lemons, juiced

1 tablespoon water

Up to 8oz/227g caster sugar

Preheat the oven and line the cake tin with greaseproof paper.

For the cake

Destone and slice the plums, then place to one side. Mix together the margarine and caster sugar on a high speed until light and fluffy. Add one egg at a time, adding a little flour in between each egg to avoid the mixture splitting. Add the vanilla extract, milk, the rest of the flour and the baking powder, and mix well.

Pour half of the mixture into the prepared tin, then place a layer of plum slices over the top. Add the rest of the mixture and top with the rest of the plum slices. Bake for 45 minutes or until a skewer comes out clean.

For the crunch topping

In a bowl, mix together the lemon juice, water and enough sugar to get a wet but thick consistency. Add to the top of the cake while the cake is still hot and leave the cake to cool completely in the tin.

RED VELVET CAKE

To perfect this recipe, we baked the cake over and over again every day for two weeks. The end result is definitely worth it. The cake has a smooth, rich, chocolatey taste that makes this a hugely popular choice for wedding cakes, and the colour you achieve at the end is really striking.

OVEN TEMPERATURE 170°C/150°C FAN OVEN | 9 INCH/23CM TIN
BAKING TIME 1 HOUR 5 MINUTES | SERVES TWELVE

4oz/113g margarine

12oz/340g caster sugar

2 eggs

8fl oz/227ml vegetable oil

1 teaspoon white vinegar

2 teaspoons vanilla extract

8fl oz/227ml buttermilk

1-2 teaspoons red gel food colouring

14oz/397g plain flour

1 heaped tablespoon cocoa powder

1 teaspoon bicarbonate of soda

Preheat the oven and line the base of the cake tin with greaseproof paper.

In a mixing bowl, cream together the margarine and sugar until pale and fluffy. Add one egg at a time, mixing well after each addition, scraping down the sides of the bowl.

Add the oil, vinegar and vanilla extract to the mixture. In a separate jug, combine the buttermilk with the food colouring, mixing until the colour has completely blended. Add small amounts of the buttermilk and the dry ingredients alternately until all of the ingredients have been added. Avoid overmixing.

Pour into the prepared tin and place into the oven, baking for 1 hour 5 minutes or until a skewer comes out clean. Once cooled completely, slice the cake in half and add either white chocolate icing or cream cheese icing (recipes on page 120).

Hints and tips

Buttermilk is essential and cannot be substituted with milk. Red food gel provides a much stronger colour than liquid food colouring.

RHUBARB AND ALMOND CAKE

The sharpness and sweetness of the rhubarb combined with almond tastes incredible. With the addition of custard icing, it makes for the perfect dessert in cake form.

OVEN TEMPERATURE 170°C/150°C FAN OVEN | 9 INCH/23CM ROUND TIN
BAKING TIME 1 HOUR 25 MINUTES | SERVES TEN

For the cake:

12oz/340g rhubarb

Splash of orange juice

Drizzle of honey

10oz/283g margarine

10oz/293g caster sugar

4 eggs

6oz/170g self-raising flour

12oz/340g ground almonds

2 teaspoons baking powder

3 tablespoons flaked almonds

Sprinkle of Demerara sugar

To finish:

Custard icing (recipe on page 121)

Preheat the oven and line the base of the tin with greaseproof paper.

For the cake

Cut the rhubarb into 3 inch sections, place onto a baking tray and cover with a splash of orange juice and honey. Cook in the oven for 8-10 minutes. Once cooked, allow to cool and then drain the rhubarb pieces in a sieve, keeping the juices to one side.

Cream together the margarine and sugar until light and fluffy. Beat in the eggs one at a time, adding a little flour in between to avoid splitting. Add the rest of the flour, the ground almonds and baking powder and mix well.

Pour half of the mixture into the prepared tin, and add half the rhubarb pieces in a circle following the curve of the tin. Add the remaining mixture and then top with the rest of the rhubarb pieces, pressing them in to the mixture to keep the top flat and avoid any burnt bits. Sprinkle over the flaked almonds and Demerara sugar. Bake the cake for 1 hour and 25 minutes, or until a skewer comes out clean. Leave to cool and remove from the tin.

To finish

For an added hit of flavour, drizzle a dash of the rhubarb cooking juice over the cake once it's baked and still hot from the oven. The juices will soak into the cake and enhance the rhubarb flavour. Slice the cake in half, spread a thick layer of custard icing over the bottom layer and place the top part of the cake back on. Place the cake into the fridge to set the icing and then enjoy.

SNICKERS BISCUIT BAR

Peanuts, biscuits, chocolate and caramel. What's not to love? If nuts aren't your thing then just use Maltesers or another of your favourite treats instead. The possibilities really are endless with this recipe.

9½X13½ INCH/24X34CM RECTANGULAR CAKE TIN
CHILLING TIME 4 HOURS | SERVES SIXTEEN

7oz/198g butter

14oz/397g milk chocolate

6 tablespoons golden syrup

1lb 12oz/794g digestive biscuits

Large handful of peanuts

3 Snickers

For the chocolate ganache:

11oz/312g chocolate

11fl oz/312ml double cream

To finish:

4 tablespoons caramel sauce
(recipe on page 122)

In a pan over a medium heat, melt the butter, chocolate and syrup. When it's completely melted, remove from the heat. In a separate bowl, crush the biscuits and then add them to the melted mixture. Mix with a wooden spoon until the biscuits are covered and then pour into the tin. Press down hard with the wooden spoon to make sure there are no air holes. Sprinkle over a layer of peanuts, then slice the Snickers and spread over the pressed mixture.

For the chocolate ganache

Make the ganache by melting the chocolate and cream in a bowl over a pan of boiling water, stirring well. When it's completely melted, pour into the tin.

To finish

Add the caramel sauce to the top and then draw a round-bladed knife or spoon through the topping to create a pattern if you like. Place in the fridge and allow to cool for a minimum of 4 hours. Remove from the tin and slice.

'WENDY'S WORLD' BROWNIES

During the making of this book, we lost a longstanding and beloved family friend, Wendy Irvine. Wendy was the type of lady whose smile would brighten any room, and she was often in her own world, but if you were to ever visit the Irvine household, these brownies would be fresh out the oven to welcome you. We had to include them as they really are out of this world; clearly a recipe that could only have come from 'Wendy's World'.

OVEN TEMPERATURE 170°C/150°C FAN OVEN | 9 INCH/23CM BAKING TIN
BAKING TIME 35 MINUTES | SERVES SIX

6oz/170g chocolate, dark chocolate is best

6oz/170g butter

9oz/255g caster sugar

3 eggs

1 tablespoon coffee essence

1 tablespoon vanilla essence

5oz/142g self-raising flour

4oz/113g chocolate chips or walnuts, chopped (optional)

Preheat the oven and line the tin.

Melt the butter and chocolate in a bowl over a pan of hot water. Leave to cool.

In a separate bowl, mix the sugar and eggs together with a whisk until light and fluffy. Stir in the flour. Add the coffee essence and vanilla essence to the mixture and mix well.

Add the melted chocolate mixture and keep whisking. If using, fold the chocolate chips or chopped walnuts into the mixture.

Transfer the brownie mixture into the prepared tin and bake in the preheated oven for 35 minutes.

WHITE CHOCOLATE AND RASPBERRY CAKE

This cake has such an awesome combination of flavours and is a firm favourite of youngest daughter Anna's. The smoothness of the white chocolate and the sharp fresh flavour of the raspberries match each other perfectly.

OVEN TEMPERATURE 170°C/150°C FAN OVEN | 9 INCH/23CM TIN
BAKING TIME 1 HOUR 5 MINUTES | SERVES TEN TO TWELVE

12oz/340g margarine

12oz/340g caster sugar

5 eggs

12oz/340g self-raising flour

1 tablespoon white chocolate powder (we use Options white hot chocolate powder)

Handful of raspberries, fresh or frozen

To finish:

White chocolate icing (recipe on page 120)

Raspberry jam

Preheat the oven and line the cake tin with greaseproof paper. Cream together the margarine and sugar, beating on a high speed until the mixture is light and fluffy. Scrape down the sides of the bowl as it's beating to make sure it's fully mixed. Add the eggs, two at a time, on a high power. Reduce the speed and add a little flour in between the eggs, then slowly increase the speed again and repeat until all of the eggs and flour are mixed.

Add the white chocolate powder and mix well. Pour into the tin and sprinkle the raspberries over the top of the mixture and gently press them in, making sure they're completely covered. Bake for 1 hour 5 minutes or until a skewer comes out clean. Wait until the cake is completely cool before removing from the tin.

To finish

Once cool, slice the cake in half and spread a layer of white chocolate icing and a layer of raspberry jam over the cake. Place the top half of the cake back on and add another layer of icing. Use a palette knife to spread the icing over the entire cake.

Fresh raspberries, fresh mint, edible flowers and dried flowers are all perfect additions to the top of this cake. (See page 126 for ideas.)

WILDFLOWER HONEY CAKE

Although this is one of our trickier recipes, it's also one of the best. Honey cake is traditionally well-known for being a Jewish wedding cake, so it tastes simply exquisite.

OVEN TEMPERATURE 180°C/160°C FAN | 9 INCH/23CM TIN (AVOID LOOSE-BOTTOMED TINS AS THE MIXTURE IS VERY WET) | BAKING TIME 1 HOUR | SERVES TEN

9oz/255g self-raising flour

8oz/227g caster sugar

1 teaspoon cinnamon

1 heaped teaspoon bicarbonate of soda

3 eggs

10oz/283g wildflower honey

8fl oz/227ml sunflower oil

8fl oz/227ml water

For the topping:

5 tablespoons wildflower honey

Line the base of the cake tin with greaseproof paper and preheat the oven.

Place all of the dry ingredients into a mixer, adding the egg and honey on a medium speed. Once the dry ingredients are evenly mixed, slowly add the oil and water on a slow speed.

Pour into the cake tin and bake for approximately 1 hour, or until a skewer comes out clean.

For the topping

Drizzle the honey over the cake while it's still hot, then leave to cool completely before removing from the tin.

Hints and tips

You can use any type of honey, but sunflower oil is necessary as any other oil will make the cake sink. Adding the honey to the cake while it's still warm will help it soak through the cake. Don't worry if the cake does sink in the middle; it still tastes delicious!

FREE FROM

This range was added to as demand grew and grew. Carol took great pride in creating these delicious recipes, and our passion to know exactly what's in our food went into all of them too. It was wonderful to provide customers who had different dietary requirements with treats and homemade food that was just as delicious as anything that does contain gluten and dairy.

CHOCOLATE FUDGE CAKE

This is a seriously good cake, rich and gooey just like a brownie and well worth the effort. It also freezes well even with the ganache on; you can freeze it in portions and defrost whenever a need for chocolate cake arises! Warm it up for a melted topping and the perfect winter warmer.

OVEN TEMPERATURE 160°C/140°C FAN OVEN | 8 INCH/20CM DEEP-SIDED CAKE TIN
BAKING TIME 1 HOUR 30 MINUTES | SERVES EIGHT

7oz/198g good quality dairy-free dark chocolate

7oz/198g dairy-free spread

1 tablespoon instant coffee granules mixed with 4fl oz/113ml cold water

3oz/85g wheat and gluten-free plain flour

3oz/85g wheat and gluten-free self-raising flour

1 teaspoon xanthan gum

¼ teaspoon bicarbonate of soda

7oz/198g light brown sugar

7oz/198g caster sugar

1oz/28g cocoa powder

2½fl oz/75ml soya, rice, or almond milk

½ tablespoon lemon juice

3 large eggs, beaten

For the ganache:

7½oz/215g good quality dairy-free dark chocolate

4fl oz/113ml gluten-free and dairy-free single cream

Preheat the oven and line the cake tin with baking parchment. Warm the chocolate, dairy-free spread and coffee over a medium heat in a heavy-based saucepan until everything has just melted; do not boil the mixture. Set aside.

In a big bowl, mix the flours, xanthan gum, bicarbonate of soda, sugars and cocoa powder, removing any lumps in the cocoa powder and brown sugar.

Heat the milk in the microwave on high power for about 20 seconds and then add the lemon juice. Stir until the milk begins to thicken and curdle. Beat the eggs in a separate bowl and then add the dairy-free milk mixture.

Add the melted chocolate mixture and the egg and milk mixture into the dry ingredients. Combine thoroughly until the cake batter is a smooth, runny consistency. Pour into the prepared cake tin and bake in the preheated oven for 1 hour 15 minutes to 1 hour 30 minutes, or until skewer comes out clean. Leave to cool for at least 1 hour before adding the topping.

For the ganache

Melt the chocolate in a heatproof bowl over a pan of boiling water. Once melted, add the dairy-free cream and stir until well combined. Pour the ganache over the cooled cake and then refrigerate to set the ganache. When set, carefully portion and wrap the cake then place into the freezer if you are making it ahead of time, or serve and enjoy straightaway.

GREEK HONEY AND PINE NUT CAKE

For mum Carol, pine nuts are a real favourite, so this cake is a particular delight. Drenched in honey with a nutty texture, it also happens to be both gluten and dairy-free. It's delicious served warm with dairy-free ice cream; there are some great options available today.

OVEN TEMPERATURE 170°C/150°C FAN | 8 INCH/20CM DEEP-SIDED ROUND TIN
BAKING TIME 50 MINUTES | SERVES EIGHT

1 tablespoon pine nuts

4oz/113g dairy-free spread

3oz/85g caster sugar

3oz/85g runny honey

1 orange, zested

2 large eggs, beaten

6oz/170g wheat and gluten-free plain flour

1 teaspoon gluten-free baking powder

¼ teaspoon bicarbonate of soda

1 teaspoon cinnamon

1 teaspoon xanthan gum

2½fl oz/74ml soya, rice, or almond milk

2oz/57g ground rice

For the orange syrup:

2 tablespoons runny honey

1 orange, juiced

Preheat the oven and line the bottom of the cake tin with baking parchment.

Toast the pine nuts on a baking tray under the grill, keeping your eye on them as they burn easily. Leave to cool. Cream the dairy-free spread, caster sugar, honey, and orange zest together until light and fluffy. Gradually add the eggs one at a time, and don't worry if the mixture curdles slightly. Sift the flour, baking powder, bicarbonate of soda, cinnamon and xanthan gum into the mixture then slowly fold in so you don't knock the air out. Slowly fold in half of the milk, then the ground rice and the remaining half of the milk. Spoon the mixture into the prepared tin, levelling the surface with the back of the spoon and then making a dip in the middle to get a level rise. Scatter over the toasted pine nuts and bake the cake for 45 to 50 minutes until slightly risen, golden and firm to the touch.

For the orange syrup

In a saucepan, mix the honey and fresh orange juice together and slowly bring to the boil. Simmer for 5 minutes without stirring, until the syrup coats the back of a wooden spoon.

As soon as the cake is out of the oven, pour the syrup over the top and leave the cake in the tin until the syrup has soaked in and the cake has cooled completely, before turning it out onto a cooling rack. This cake freezes well and is also lovely served warm with a scoop or two of dairy-free ice cream.

LEMON AND POPPY SEED SYRUP CAKE

A fantastic and versatile recipe. Bake this one for your friends and see if they can even tell it's gluten and dairy-free! A perfect cake for a light afternoon treat.

OVEN TEMPERATURE 180°C/160°C FAN | 8 INCH/20CM LOOSE-BOTTOMED DEEP TIN
BAKING TIME 1 HOUR | SERVES EIGHT

8oz/227g dairy-free spread

8oz/227g caster sugar

2 lemons, zested and juiced

4 eggs

8oz/227g gluten and wheat-free self-raising flour

1 teaspoon xanthan gum

2 tablespoons blue poppy seeds

For the lemon syrup:

Juice from the two lemons

6oz/170g caster sugar

3fl oz/85ml water

Preheat the oven and line the cake tin with baking parchment. Cream the dairy-free spread, sugar and lemon zest until light and fluffy. Add one egg at a time, making sure everything is thoroughly combined after each addition. Don't worry if the mixture curdles slightly. Add the flour, xanthan gum and blue poppy seeds one tablespoon at a time and mix well. Spoon the mixture into the prepared cake tin and then bake for 1 hour or until a skewer inserted into the centre of the cake comes out clean.

For the lemon syrup

In a saucepan, mix the lemon juice, caster sugar and water together. Slowly bring to the boil and simmer for 5 minutes without stirring, until the syrup coats the back of a wooden spoon. As soon as the cake is out of the oven, pour the syrup over the cake and leave it in the tin until the syrup has soaked in and the cake has cooled completely.

RASPBERRY AND ALMOND CAKE

Raspberries and almonds are a match made in heaven, especially when you're baking with them – the aroma is just heavenly – but the best thing about this award-winning cake is that nobody guesses it's gluten and dairy-free. This cake was awarded 'Best Free From Product 2017' by Deliciously Yorkshire.

OVEN TEMPERATURE 180°C/160°C FAN | 8 INCH/20CM DEEP-SIDED ROUND TIN
BAKING TIME 1 HOUR 15 MINUTES | SERVES EIGHT

6oz/170g dairy-free spread

6oz/170g caster sugar

½ teaspoon vanilla extract

3 large eggs

3oz/85g wheat and gluten-free self-raising flour

1 teaspoon xanthan gum

½ teaspoon gluten-free baking powder

4oz/113g ground almonds

6oz/170g fresh or frozen raspberries

Preheat the oven and line the base with baking parchment.

Cream the dairy-free spread, caster sugar and vanilla extract together until light and fluffy. Gradually add the eggs one at a time. Don't worry if the mixture starts to curdle. Slowly fold in the flour, xanthan gum, baking powder and ground almonds, taking care not to knock out the air. Gently fold in the raspberries, taking care not to break them up. Spoon the mixture into the prepared tin and level out with the back of a spoon.

Bake for 1 hour to 1 hour 15 minutes, or until a skewer comes out clean from the centre of the cake. Remove the cake from the oven and leave to cool. Dust with icing sugar just before serving.

This cake is delicious with dairy free ice cream, and freezes well if you're not going to eat it on the day.

VEGAN BANANA, RAISIN AND PEANUT NIB CAKE

With this cake, each core ingredient complements the next, with bananas adding flavour, raisins adding moisture and peanut nibs adding texture.

OVEN TEMPERATURE 160°C/140°C FAN | 2LB LOAF TIN
BAKING TIME 45-50 MINUTES | SERVES TWELVE

8½oz/240g plain flour
1½ teaspoons baking powder
½ teaspoon salt
7oz/198g caster sugar
2fl oz/57ml vegetable oil
4 ripe bananas, mashed
2fl oz/57ml cold water
1 teaspoon vanilla paste
3½oz/100g raisins (optional)
60g peanut nibs (optional)

Preheat the oven and line the base of the loaf tin with parchment paper.

In a small bowl, combine the flour, baking powder and salt. In a separate bowl, whisk together the sugar and oil, then add the mashed bananas. Add the water and vanilla to the banana mixture and stir to combine. Add the flour mixture and stir until none of the flour is visible. Stir in the raisins and peanut nibs, setting some aside for decoration, then transfer the mixture into the prepared tin and bake for 45 to 50 minutes or until skewer comes out clean.

Leave to cool, decorate with the remaining sultanas and peanut nibs, and enjoy.

VEGAN CARROT CAKE

We love carrot cake here at Jervaulx. Not only is it unbelievably tasty, you can convince yourself you're eating something healthy; it does have veggies in after all!

OVEN TEMPERATURE 160°C/140°C FAN | 8 INCH/20CM DEEP CAKE TIN
BAKING TIME 45 MINUTES | SERVES EIGHT

1lb 2oz/510g plain flour

½ teaspoon salt

2 teaspoons baking powder

½ teaspoon bicarbonate of soda

1 teaspoon cinnamon

3½oz/100g raisins

3½oz/100g walnuts (optional)

10½oz/300g carrots, peeled and grated

5fl oz/142ml corn oil

4fl oz/113ml fresh orange juice

9oz/255g caster sugar

Preheat the oven and line the cake tin.

Mix the flour, salt, baking powder, bicarbonate of soda, cinnamon, raisins and walnuts (if using) together in a large bowl. Add the carrots and oil to the dry ingredients and mix everything together using a wooden spoon. Once that's well combined, add the orange juice and sugar and stir thoroughly, making sure there are no lumps of carrot remaining. Carefully spoon the mixture into the prepared tin and bake for 45 minutes or until a skewer comes out clean. Leave the cake to cool for 30 minutes before turning out onto a plate or cake stand.

VEGAN CHOCOLATE CAKE WITH ROASTED CACAO NIBS AND PISTACHIO NUTS

This is a delicious, decadent chocolate cake that tastes wonderful and just so happens to be vegan.

OVEN TEMPERATURE 180°C/160°C FAN | 8 INCH/20CM DEEP SPRING FORM CAKE TIN
BAKING TIME 50 MINUTES | SERVES TWELVE

1 tablespoon lemon juice

11fl oz/312ml dairy-free milk (we use soya or almond)

5oz/142g dairy-free margarine

3 tablespoons golden, agave or maple syrup (maple syrup will make this cake less sweet)

1 teaspoon instant coffee granules

10oz/283g self-raising flour

6oz/170g granulated sugar

4 tablespoons unsweetened cocoa powder

1 teaspoon bicarbonate of soda

1oz/28g roasted cacao nibs (optional)

2oz/57g ground pistachio nuts (optional)

For the topping:

2½oz/75g dairy-free margarine

7oz/198g icing sugar

4 tablespoons cocoa powder

2 tablespoons water

2oz/57g ground pistachio nuts

Dried roses

Preheat the oven and line the cake tin with baking parchment. Stir the lemon juice into the milk and set aside. In a heavy-based pan over a medium heat, melt the margarine, syrup and coffee together and set aside to cool slightly. Put the flour, sugar, cocoa powder, and bicarbonate of soda into a large bowl and pour the milk and melted margarine mixture over the flour mixture, stirring well until it becomes a smooth batter. Stir in the cacao nibs and pistachio nuts if using. Transfer the batter into the prepared tin and bake for 50 minutes or until a skewer comes out clean. Leave to cool before icing.

For the vegan chocolate topping

While the cake is in the oven, beat the margarine, icing sugar, cocoa powder and water together until smooth. When the cake is completely cool, spread the topping onto the top of the cake and then decorate with pistachio nuts and dried roses. You could also slice the cake in half and use the topping to fill it as well.

VEGAN CHOCOLATE POT

Vegan as well as gluten-free, this is a great little pudding you can serve on its own or topped with fruit. While it's still warm you could even pour it over a cake! Youngest daughter Anna adores this dessert, so we usually make a few extra pots just in case some go missing…

PREPARATION TIME 20 MINUTES, PLUS 2 HOURS CHILLING | SERVES FOUR TO SIX

3 tablespoons cornflour

2oz/65g caster sugar

1oz/28g cocoa powder

Pinch of salt

17fl oz/482ml plain unsweetened almond milk

25g bag of dairy-free chocolate chips

½ teaspoon vanilla paste

In a small bowl, combine the cornflour with two tablespoons of cold water and mix until you have a thin paste. In a small pan, combine the sugar, cocoa powder and salt. Over a medium to low heat, gradually add the almond milk, stirring constantly until smooth. Cook until a thin film develops on top of the liquid and steam rises from the surface, but do not let the mixture boil. Remove the pan from the heat and add the chocolate chips, stirring constantly with a wooden spoon until the chocolate chips have melted. Stir in the cornflour mixture and vanilla paste, return to the heat and, stirring constantly, cook until the mixture thickens but is still thinner than required. The pudding will thicken as it cools. Transfer into the prepared pudding dishes, and cover with cling film to prevent a skin forming. Put in the fridge to cool and decorate with fruit before serving.

RELISHES

Our range of preserves was inspired by local produce and a desire to make everything we could ourselves for the tearoom. It's important to us to know what's in our food and where it comes from, so making these easy preserves from scratch is a winner all round.

The only thing to remember is to sterilise your jars and lids before using them to store preserves, which you can easily do at home by following these steps:

Wash your jars in warm soapy water, rinse thoroughly, and then leave to dry naturally on a clean cloth or surface.

30 minutes before the pickle or relish is ready, place the jars on a baking tray and into a cold oven. Set the temperature to 140°C and leave the jars in the oven until needed.

To sterilise the lids, place them into boiling water for 10 minutes, and then leave to dry naturally on a clean cloth or surface.

BEETROOT RELISH

This is such a versatile relish; it can be served on your favourite burgers or sausages, is delicious with salads, chicken and fish, and makes a perfect accompaniment to cheese and crackers or simply fresh bread. Adding it to a cheese sandwich for a kick of flavour is our favourite.

PREPARATION TIME APPROXIMATELY 1 HOUR 30 MINUTES

35oz/1kg raw beetroot
25oz/750g red or white onions
25oz/750g cooking apples
17fl oz/510ml white wine vinegar
17oz/510g soft brown sugar
2 tablespoons ginger, peeled and grated
2 cloves of garlic, peeled and crushed
2 teaspoons ground cinnamon
1 heaped teaspoon turmeric
2 teaspoons paprika, or cayenne pepper if you want a bit of bite

Start by peeling and then coarsely grating the beetroot, apple and onion in the food processor. Measure out all the other ingredients. Put all the ingredients into a large heavy-based pan and heat the mixture until it's boiling. Reduce to a simmer, uncovered, for about 1 hour 30 minutes, stirring occasionally with a wooden spoon, until the beetroot is tender, and the liquid has reduced to a syrupy consistency.

Transfer the relish into warm sterilised jars and seal with a lid. Once sealed the beetroot relish will keep for a few months.

CRUNCHY PICCALILLI

Piccalilli is an English interpretation of Indian pickles, a relish made with chopped pickled vegetables and spices. A great accompaniment for cheese and cooked meats.

PREPARATION TIME 1 HOUR, PLUS 24 HOURS PICKLING

1 large broccoli

1 large cauliflower

3 medium-sized onions, diced into 1cm cubes

2 large courgettes, deseeded and diced into 1cm cubes

7oz/198g fine beans, sliced

3½oz/100g salt

3oz/85g plain flour, sieved

½oz/14g mild curry powder

½oz/14g turmeric

3oz/85g wholegrain mustard

1oz/28g ground ginger

1¾ pints/1 litre white wine vinegar

20oz/567g caster sugar

Break the broccoli and cauliflower into florets and dice the stalks. Place all the prepared vegetables in a large bowl, toss in the salt, and leave for 24 hours.

Rinse very thoroughly in several changes of water until the salt has been completely washed away. Drain well and leave for at least 30 minutes.

Put the sieved flour and spices into a large heavy-based pan and gradually add the vinegar, blending well to a smooth paste with no lumps. Add the rest of the vinegar and the sugar and bring to the boil, stirring all the time until the mixture is thick. Add the prepared vegetables and bring back to the boil, continuing to stir so the piccalilli doesn't stick and burn on the bottom. Remove from the heat and transfer into warm sterile jars. Seal with the lid and leave the piccalilli for 1 month to mature, if you can resist it that long!

SWEET CHILLI JAM

Our sweet chilli jam is brilliant on bean burgers, with halloumi, or as an ingredient in dressings.

PREPARATION TIME 30 MINUTES

3 red chillies, deseeded if you want a milder jam

3 cloves of garlic, peeled

2½cm piece fresh ginger, peeled

7oz/198g caster sugar

400g tin chopped tomatoes

2fl oz/57ml white wine vinegar

Whizz the chillies, garlic and ginger in a food processor until they become a paste. Spoon the paste into a heavy-based pan and add the sugar, tomatoes and vinegar. Bring to the boil then turn the heat down to a simmer and cook the jam for 20-25 minutes until thick and glossy.

Pour into warm sterilised jars and seal.

The jam will keep for a year unopened, and once opened it should be good for a few weeks kept in the fridge.

HOMEMADE AT
JERVAULX
ABBEY

Chilli Jam

Fresh red chilli
jam to liven up
your taste buds "

WENSLEYDALE BEER AND APPLE CHUTNEY

Delicious, fruity and a perfect match for meats and cheeses. You can use your favourite beer or ale; Wensleydale Brewery Gamekeeper's Best Bitter is a 'light copper, very drinkable and highly moreish' ale, brewed with crystal malt and magnum hops at our local brewery in Leyburn, which creates a juicy flavour that partners really well with apples and dates in our punchy chutney.

PREPARATION TIME: 1 HOUR

6fl oz/170ml white wine vinegar

10oz/283g light brown sugar

17½fl oz/500ml Wensleydale Gamekeeper's Best Bitter

2lb/907g eating apples, peeled, cored and diced

1lb/454g onions, diced

8oz/227g dates, chopped

4 teaspoons mustard seeds

2 teaspoons ginger purée

1 teaspoon sea salt

1 teaspoon cayenne pepper

Put the white wine vinegar and sugar in a large heavy-based pan on a medium heat to dissolve the sugar. Once the sugar has fully dissolved, add the remaining ingredients. Bring to the boil, turn down the heat and simmer for 50 minutes or until the chutney thickens and the fruit has softened.

Use this time to sterilise your jars and lids.

Once the chutney has thickened, fill the jars and seal with a lid. This chutney is great once cooled but gets even better kept. The chutney will keep for a year unopened, and once opened it should be good for a few weeks kept in the fridge.

FINISHING TOUCHES

Follow our hints and tips to transform your bakes into fantastic creations that will impress and delight whoever you're celebrating with. Along with icings and sauces to add an extra layer of indulgence to your cakes, you can also use edible flowers, herbs, and fresh fruits – many of which are easy to grow in your own garden – to turn any bake into something really special.

CLASSIC VANILLA CUPCAKES

Vanilla cupcakes are an absolute classic. They're amazing just as they are, or they can be made as fancy as you like by changing the flavours, decoration or even adding jam into the middle. The finishing touches turn this humble cupcake into a stunning creation that can be enjoyed by everyone.

OVEN TEMPERATURE 170°C/150°C FAN OVEN | CUPCAKE TIN
BAKING TIME 15-20 MINUTES | MAKES SIXTEEN

8oz/227g margarine
8oz/227g caster sugar
3 eggs
2 tablespoons vanilla extract
8oz/227g self-raising flour

Preheat the oven.

Cream together the margarine and sugar, beating on a high speed until the mixture is light and fluffy. Scrape down the sides of the bowl as it's beating to make sure it's fully mixed. Add the eggs, two at a time, and vanilla extract on a high power. Reduce the speed and add a little flour in between the eggs, then slowly increase the speed again and repeat until all of the eggs and flour are mixed.

Beat for couple of minutes to ensure everything is thoroughly combined before evenly distributing into cupcake cases. The amount you put into each case is important; a rounded tablespoon should be perfect. The cupcake case should be half or just below half full.

Bake for 15-20 minutes. The cupcakes should rise to the top of the cases.

To finish

Choose an icing to top off your creation (recipes on page 120). Vanilla buttercream is our favourite! Use a piping bag to create your topping and decorate with fresh fruits and edible flowers.

Variations

To make chocolate cupcakes, swap 2oz/57g of flour for cocoa powder and don't add any vanilla extract. For the chocolate icing, (See page 120). Finish off with mini chocolates or decorations of your choice.

To make lemon icing add the zest from four lemons. Add lemon curd in a piping bag and squeeze into the centre of the cupcake.

MINI CAKES

These ones are blueberry and lemon flavour but you can experiment with different ingredients to make your own favourite mini cakes.

OVEN TEMPERATURE 150°C | 9½X13½ INCH/24X34CM RECTANGULAR CAKE TIN
BAKING TIME 1 HOUR | SERVES SIX

1lb/454g margarine

1lb/454g caster sugar

6 eggs

1lb/454g self-raising flour

3 lemons, zested

7oz/198g blueberries

To finish:

Butter icing (recipe on page 120)

Preheat the oven and grease and line your cake tin.

Cream together the margarine and sugar, beating on a high speed until the mixture is light and fluffy. Scrape down the sides of the bowl as it's beating to make sure it's fully mixed. Add the eggs, two at a time, on a high power. Reduce the speed and add a little flour in between the eggs, then slowly increase the speed again and repeat until all of the eggs and flour are mixed. Add the lemon zest. Pour the cake batter into the lined tin, spread the blueberries evenly over the top, and bake for approximately 1 hour, or until a skewer comes out clean.

To finish

Once completely cooled, slice through the cake to make each half 2½cm tall. Using a 3cm deep by 7.5cm wide cutter, cut out 12 rounds. Put your butter icing into a piping bag and try out different shaped piping nozzles on some baking paper first. When you have found an effect you like, pipe the butter icing onto the top of each layer, going around the edge first and then moving into the middle. We have made them two tiers high. Place the top layer on and decorate as desired.

BUTTER ICING

This will make enough icing to cover any of the cakes in this book, although you may be left with a little extra for some recipes. As a general rule, if you're just filling the cake or icing cupcakes, halve this recipe. If you are icing the whole cake you will need the full amount.

1lb/454g butter, at room temperature

1lb/454g icing sugar

Variations:

10ml vanilla extract

20ml elderflower cordial

4oz/113g cocoa powder

1 tablespoon Options white hot chocolate powder

Beat the butter with the icing sugar, starting off slowly to avoid icing sugar flying out, and gaining speed until on full power. Then add a splash of liquid, such as water or milk, and beat again until the icing becomes paler in colour, usually 3 to 5 minutes.

Variations

For vanilla icing, add vanilla extract at the same point as the liquid. For elderflower icing, add elderflower cordial at the same point as the liquid.

For chocolate icing, add cocoa powder with the icing sugar. We use Bournville as it's a beautifully rich cocoa powder. Avoid hot chocolate powders.

For white chocolate butter icing, add white hot chocolate powder with the icing sugar. We use Options hot white chocolate for the best flavour.

CREAM CHEESE ICING

8oz/227g cream cheese, chilled

8oz/227g butter, at room temperature

16oz/450g icing sugar

Beat all of the ingredients together for 3 to 5 minutes on high speed until pale. Make sure all the butter has been incorporated properly.

CHOCOLATE GANACHE

This will make enough icing to cover any of the cakes in this book, although you may be left with a little extra for some recipes. As a general rule, if you're just filling the cake or icing cupcakes, halve this recipe. If you are icing the whole cake you will need the full amount.

7oz/198g milk chocolate

4fl oz/113ml cream

Variations:

10oz/283g white chocolate

7fl oz/198ml cream

Melt the chocolate in a bowl over hot water, then remove from the heat and add the cream. Stir with a spatula until it's completely smooth. The consistency should be dripping off the spoon, not running. If it's too warm, it will run straight down the side of the cake. Refrigerate for a few minutes and stir until the consistency is correct. You can use a tablespoon or a pouring jug to create the drips by slowly pouring around the edge of cake, and then continuing into the centre of the cake to cover the whole top.

Variations:

For a white chocolate ganache, melt the cream and chocolate together in a bowl over a pan of hot water. Stir until all the chocolate has melted.

CUSTARD ICING

6oz/170g butter, at room temperature

13oz/369g icing sugar

1oz/28g custard powder

1fl oz/28ml milk

Add all of the ingredients to a mixing bowl and beat together for 5-10 minutes. Beat well to ensure the custard powder has been completely mixed and you can't taste or feel any graininess. For a creamy taste, leave in the fridge overnight. Remove from the fridge and allow the icing to warm to room temperature. Mix well again and begin to ice your cake.

SALTED CARAMEL SAUCE

If you haven't made caramel sauce before, don't be scared. You do need to pay close attention to the caramel. With a little care, you can make the most amazing homemade salted caramel sauce. Homemade caramel can be achieved but it may take a little practice. It needs preparation and attention; it's all about timings and maybe a few lessons learned along the way. Make sure all your ingredients are ready and at hand. Once you've mastered it, you won't regret it; the results are irresistible.

8oz/227g unsalted butter, at room temperature

14oz/397g granulated sugar

8fl oz/227ml double cream, at room temperature

1 tablespoon fleur de sel or sea salt

Firstly, make sure you have all the ingredients ready and cube the butter. To begin, heat the sugar over a medium-high heat in the bottom of a large, heavy saucepan. When the sugar starts to melt, start to move the pan around. The sugar will clump up, but keep swirling the pan and it will continue to melt. Do not stir the sugar with a spoon or whisk at this point, gently swirl the whole pan. When the sugar has melted, stop moving the pan. Continue cooking the sugar until it reaches a deep amber colour. Make sure you watch the pan very closely as this is where it is easy to burn the caramel. As soon as the sugar reaches a dark amber colour, carefully add the butter and whisk until it's melted. Remove the pan from the heat and slowly pour in the cream. Whisk until the cream is completely incorporated and the caramel is smooth, then add the fleur de sel or sea salt flakes.

Let the caramel sauce cool for about 10 minutes in the pan, then pour the caramel into a large jar and cool to room temperature. Put the salted caramel sauce in the refrigerator. It can be stored in there for about a month.

ICING STYLES

NAKED CAKE

To achieve the best results, bake two cakes and slice them evenly into 1 inch slices, making four layers. For the cake recipe turn to page 82.

Place the first cake layer onto a turntable and put your chosen icing into piping bag. Pipe a layer of icing on top of the cake layer, starting around the edge and finishing in the middle. Add a layer of jam, caramel or lemon curd, whichever suits your cake. Place another cake layer on top and repeat. Leave the sides and the very top of the cake completely bare. When all four layers are done, you will have achieved the naked cake look, and can choose fresh fruits and edible flowers to decorate.

SEMI-NAKED CAKE

This style can be achieved with any butter icing, although a white icing is more effective. Using a turntable is also essential. For the cake recipe turn to page 74.

Slice your cakes, top each with a nice layer of icing and stack the cake on the turntable. Add enough butter icing to completely cover the cake to the very top, and with a flat spatula spread the icing over the top and sides. The trick is to add more than you need and remove the icing with a flat scraping tool. While turning the cake, use a flat edged blade or scraper around the sides of the cake to remove excess icing until the finished look has been achieved.

OMBRE ICING

This is a lovely effect that can really make your cake stand out. While making your butter icing, add a tiny amount of food colouring. In this instance, we chose pink. Remove some of the icing and place into a bowl, then add another drop of food colouring and mix well. Remove some of that icing and then place into another bowl, adding more food colouring and mixing to get a stronger colour. Repeat this process until you have at least four different shades.

Place the cake onto a turntable. Slice through the middle and top the bottom layer with butter icing. We added some raspberry jam for this cake; you could use lemon curd or caramel depending on the flavours and colours. Replace the top half of the cake and put your different shades of icing into different piping bags.

Start at the bottom with the darkest shade, piping at least two lines all the way around the cake. Move on to the next shade, and work your way up the cake which should get lighter as you reach the top. Continue with the lightest shade for the top of the cake so it's completely covered. Now using a flat edged blade or scraper, turn the cake and carefully remove excess icing one section at a time. The colours will merge together but always keep your blade clean, so the colours don't end up where they shouldn't. Smooth over the top of the cake, keeping the blade flat, to finish.

DRIP CAKE

Using either chocolate ganache or caramel, fully ice your cake, and then chill it in the fridge.

Whichever icing you chose first, use the other one to create the drip effect. The ganache or caramel should be slightly warm, making it a little runny. Ensure that it's not too hot as this will immediately melt your icing; just above room temperature is perfect.

Use either a spoon or a jug to start pouring the ganache or caramel around the edge on top of the cake, allowing it to flow over the edge. You're looking for an effect where the length of the drips is uneven, so don't worry if some drips allow more ganache or caramel to flow over the cake edge than others. Once you have completed the whole edge of the cake, fill in the middle but be careful not to overfill it and create more drips! Take your time with this. To get the right effect, it takes a bit of patience.

EDIBLE DECORATIONS

We love to use fresh edible flowers to make our cakes look extra special and most you can even grow in your garden. Here's a list of our favourites:

Violas – easily grown in small shrubs making them perfect for any garden. The ancient Greeks considered the viola to be a symbol of love and fertility.

Alpine pinks (dianthus) – ideal for spring and autumn planting, and really easy to grow in troughs and window boxes.

Elderflowers – grown on the elderberry tree. Blooming during spring and summer, the flower has a slight scent. The elderberry is purple-black in colour and is a great food source for birds and small animals.

Lavender – one of the most fragrant and highly versatile herbs you can grow! Lavender is used in essentials oils, medicine, food and drinks, and is also lovely for decorative purposes.

Nasturtium – known for their brightly coloured flowers, which makes them a great flower to decorate with, adding colour and fun. This plant is native to South and Central America.

Roses – red roses are a symbol of love, yellow for friendship, white for purity, pink for joy and orange for enthusiasm. Pick your colour to suit your mood!

Geraniums – often used in essential oils, these plants like it best in sun-filled areas with a rich soil.

Mint – rich in vitamins, mint is a pretty incredible plant. With many different species to choose from, each with its own characteristics, mint is used in oils as well as for medical and culinary purposes.

Fresh fruits are also a beautiful addition to any cake. Of course, you can use any fruits you wish, just think about which colours and sizes will work best with each cake.

Here are some ideas to start with: raspberries, strawberries, blueberries, fresh figs, physalis, cherries and blackberries.

Please note, we would always recommend using a professional company for edible flowers.
If you choose to grow your own, please check the Food Standards Agency website for correct and up to date instructions on growing your edible flowers.

©2018 Meze Publishing Ltd & Jervaulx Abbey
Tearoom. All rights reserved.

First edition printed in 2018 in the UK.

ISBN: 978-1-910863-37-4

*Authors: Ian Burdon, Carol Burdon,
Gayle Hussan nee Burdon, Anna Burdon*

Edited by: Katie Fisher, Phil Turner & Alana Bishop

Designed by: Paul Cocker

Photography by: Tim Green

*Contributors: Sarah Koriba, David Wilson,
Kym Du Toit, Jessica Findlow, Izzy Randall*

Published by Meze Publishing Limited
Unit 1b, 2 Kelham Square
Kelham Riverside
Sheffield S3 8SD
Web: www.mezepublishing.co.uk
Telephone: 0114 275 7709
Email: info@mezepublishing.co.uk